HAIR, GIRTH, AND RUDE AWAKENINGS

childhood, fatherhood, and the chaos in between

MICHAEL NADER

ISBN-10: 0692259724

ISBN-13: 978-0692259726

First Printing: 2014

Inspired Artistry
312 Park, Unit 7
Clarendon Hills, IL 60514

Inspired Artistry Contact:

publisher@inspired-artistry.com

DEDICATION

For J and G – I have grown gray watching you grow older. Some of the gray is your fault, but that is part of the job description. I would not trade a moment of it away. Never forget to find beauty in the simple things, nothing is just brown.

For D - thank you for bringing J and G into my life.

For my occasional reader - motivation sometimes comes from without.

Finally, for my father - who showed me that hard-work and love are qualities a man should possess.

CONTENTS

ACKNOWLEDGMENTS

I cannot begin to thank all of the people who provided guidance or inspiration on this project. Many of them, did so unknowingly. From my mother who taught me to love writing, to the random person on the street who would inspire a moment between my children and me, there are simply too many people to recognize.

Special acknowledgement, however, needs to be given to Nicolette Halenza for her help in editing. Your direct and constructive feedback was invaluable. Keep seeing the world with your writer's eye.

Finally, I would like to acknowledge my family, my friends, and colleagues (the occasional reader); who, over the years would read these stories, laugh, and encourage me to put this together.

WHY THIS EXISTS

There was a point in my life (I have to believe) when I would have showered, thoroughly, had someone just urinated on me in the middle of the night. Somewhere between the birth of your first child and the day your nest empties, your standards change. Suddenly, a simple bath with hand sanitizer (or a warm wet-wipe) is acceptable before crawling back to bed. Children have a way of altering your perceptions.

I had no intention of ever writing this book. However, having children invade your life (untreated) can lead to mental instability. As such, the essays and stories that follow are therapy of sorts. They are my way, from a seat on a plane or a quiet hotel room, of remembering why I put up with the TSA and bad room-service hamburgers. They cover a time in mine and my son's lives that saw them move from little boys to teenagers, and saw us move from Connecticut to California, and California to Illinois.

Many books about parenting speak about the beauty of children. Some also discuss the difficulty of the task of parenting. This book is more about the chaos of it. Moreover, this is not a book about parenting; it is a book about a parent. Think of it like a hard demarcation, separating the act from the insanity. Between the two, the insanity is more interesting.

Ultimately, this book became a project for my children. I wanted it to be something they could look back on (and laugh about) years from now. We all start out idolizing our parents, and then somewhere along the line we (as children) start seeing them as human. I wanted my boys to see the way this father's mind worked prior to them, and because of them. What follows, simply put, is an unprepared father's perspective on childhood and fatherhood.

SUFFERING FOR SANITY

Einstein defined insanity as repeating the same action over and over, but expecting different results. What Einstein lacks in his definition is a concrete example. As such, allow me to provide one. Insanity is being a parent. The moment your child enters your world, life will take a 90-degree turn from your linear path, and move you to a twisted road that provides little more than a few hundred feet of visibility amongst the trees, hills, and valleys. If my children have taught me anything, it is that the only way to hold onto any thread of sanity is to simply accept that you will never again see past the trees ahead until they have already hit you in the face; and, it is very possible that you might trip on a rock while you are rubbing your eyes. Come to think out it, Einstein may have been thinking of children when he spoke of insanity.

As a father you will tell your children the same things over and over – and over, and over, and over again – and you will, somehow, expect different results.

For example, realistically speaking, it simply makes sense to put your shoes by the door so you can find them, and so you do not end up wearing your mother's tennis shoes to the birthday party because they are the only available footwear visible on the premises. Fatherhood is insanity, the sooner you accept that the happier you will be.

Contrary to what you may have heard, the moment your first child is born, watching the compressed head impossibly emerge into the world (at least for the father) is not the most memorable portion of that experience. Make no mistake the image sticks in your mind for many reasons. For that matter, what follows the child from the scared orifice is altogether just as memorable, but for very different reasons. Let it suffice to say that when the doctor asks you to move, you should.

The most memorable, and terrifying, part of having a child is the drive home from the hospital. When Stan Lee created Spiderman, he must have modeled the concept of "Spidey Sense" off of the heightened, euphoric, hallucinogenic state of a second day father. Emerging from the hospital door with car seat in hand is a Matrix moment. You will see every leaf move on every tree in slow motion, you will feel every step toward the car, your fingers, like a micrometer, will feel the exact thickness of the key. I have to believe that this heightened sense of awareness has some biological underpinning, that it is an inborn genetic reaction, something telling you that this is yours to protect, and that nature is providing you with the tools you need to survive. Driving even the slowest speed feels preternatural as every car you see is an impending projectile aimed at your soul. If you have ever been level 30 of Missile Command, you know what I mean (yes, I realize this analogy dates me severely). I would like to believe that it is some innate biological instinct instead of pure fear. I realize that it is unlikely the latter – women have biological chemistry when it comes to children. Men, on the other hand, are slightly more advanced than bears.

There are those days, of course, that (as a father) you will wish you were a proud male grizzly and were able to deal with the children accordingly. When your son decides to see how long his hand can withstand ice cold liquid by opening the tap of the keg of beer you got for the party and letting it run over his trembling extremity and into the grass, nourishing no one but the roots of the California rye, you will understand the bounds of sanity and find some kernel of wisdom in the nature of the bear.

My son is of that age when every request has become a battle. From the simplest thing like, "please remove the shoe from the refrigerator," (odors are not effectively suppressed by a Frigidaire), to the complexities of completely chewing and swallowing Oreo cookies prior to brushing his teeth (you can never really get the chocolate crumbs out of the tooth brush). He is determined to fight. As this has become the pattern in my home, I have (of course) deemed it necessary to break his spirit and fight back, often about inane things, just to simply impose my will. As I said, men are as much grizzly as human (especially when it comes to emotion).

Armed with this completely irrational logic and emotion, I recently engaged in a battle with my oldest. He was watching the "big" TV in the living room. As a good general, I sized up my opponent prior to the battle. I walked into the room, got a cup of cold water (to still the nerves), and paused to observe his state. Star Wars: The Clone Wars is the opiate of the 13-year-old geek, This is a quote directly from the less famous Russian dictator. Mentally, I prepped my very rational argument (something to the effect of, "the TV is mine because I paid for it"). In an irrational mind there is a belief that fiscal arguments tend to work on 13-year-old boys.

It was time – I fired the first shot, "after the next commercial I am putting on the news." I had no intention of putting on the news, but it never hurts to add dramatic nuances to the battle. If you have ever been in a fight, you recognize that the time from the first strike to the retaliation is microscopic (assuming both combatants are prepared), but the fractions of time feel like the length of the average Don McLean song. I waited; mentally humming, "Bye, bye Miss American Pie." Then it came. my oldest simply looked at me, smiled, and said, "OK, Dad."

The commercial came; he hugged me and said, "I love you. I am sorry you have been so stressed with work." He walked upstairs, and I sat down before I fell down. For the record, that goes down as a strategic loss for me, but then, sometimes, you have to lose a battle to move forward. Patton, or someone, must have said something like that at some point.

Ultimately what I realized is that Einstein was wrong, sometimes you repeat the same action and you find that the outcome is never predetermined. I was listening to a song on my iPod the other day ("Silent Scream" by Richard Marx) and a line stood out to me:

"Memories, moments you recall, we should be remembered for the greatest of them all. You can't begin to live someone else's life, or your own will pass you by."

Of course my son is going to fight with me. He has to. He has to try to exercise some level of control over his life, his incipient adulthood. He needs to look at me and realize that he needs to move beyond both my expectations and existence. That does not mean that I will stop trying to define part of who he is, but I should not expect to ever fully succeed. What is truly insane is that I have come to find comfort in the small battles and miss them terribly when they disappear. I wonder what Einstein would say about that.

I wanted to run up the stairs and say to him that stress is a bi-product of life. Work is easy. It is the emotions you develop for those in your life that cause real stress. Love hurts as much as it heals, but the beautiful thing is that it is the great equalizer. It may keep us on the edge of sanity, but at least you can admire the world from the peaks, even the small ones – they are worth a lifetime of walking through the valleys. I wanted to tell him, but the nature of love really cannot be explained, just experienced. Instead, I sat and watched the news. He knows he threw the battle, I know he handed me a victory, but I will take it – it was far from shallow.

SCENT OF A 12-YEAR OLD

"Smell my armpits Dad."
I was sitting quietly on the couch watching TV on a lazy Saturday evening when my oldest came running down the stairs with enthusiasm generally reserved for birthdays. "Dad, smell my armpits!" This statement has now made my list of unexpected phrases. I would put it in the category of something like "please grab the duck out of the bathtub for dinner" (an equally plausible phrase, and yet something I never expect to hear).

♋

This scene needs context. My oldest and I were at the store that afternoon. To provide him with some practical knowledge, I took him to the store to help me buy groceries for the week. Truthfully, I also took him so he could help load and unload the car. Creative methods for effectively allocating (or altogether relinquishing) work is a lesson I will teach him another day.

My son does not mind going to the store. He has learned through careful deduction that longer store trips (particularly with Dad) let him sneak coveted items onto the list and into the cart. He always makes standard requests – his first being Peanut Butter Captain Crunch.

I have to pause here for a moment to state that I adore Peanut Butter Captain Crunch. If I were a condemned man I would seriously consider asking for this as part of my last meal. However, it has to be the Peanut Butter Captain Crunch of my youth not the pitiful imitation we push on the current generation. I would need the cereal that melted like cotton candy and left the milk so sticky sweet as to induce a diabetic coma simply by being in its presence. Since today's version of the cereal did not meet these peanut butter standards, I said no.

His second request, Pop-Tarts. I have no particular affection here. It is an occasional thing; I said yes. In short, Dad is a pushover at the grocery store and an enterprising 12-year-old knows this. It is a scientifically proven part of their universal genetic code. I can only take solace in the fact that I have no daughters, as I have no doubt that my inability to deny the less-than-occasional treat would spread to locations far more expensive than my local Safeway.

Once he has acquired his first treasure, the beast is much easier to tame. Not wanting to overplay his hand, normally, I can move through three or four aisles before the next ask comes into play. This was still further reason for agreeing on the Pop-Tarts. I gave those up on the sixth aisle of a twenty aisle store. Given the standard aisle ratio, I need only fend off two more serious requests on this trip. Further, one of those would come in the frozen vegetable or fresh fruit areas. Historically, vegetables are an anti-kid zone, making his unconventional choice a clear win for me.

The seeming lack of intelligence shown by two boys 10 and 12 is a ploy. It is simply an act to reel you in and hang you with your own words or actions. Being plain-spoken, coupled with the courage to speak your mind, is second nature to a child. And it is something that many of us, unfortunately, outgrow. If my children have taught me anything, it is to leave nothing unspoken. For my kids, this is less of a lesson and more a means to an end. My son broke pattern at the store. We had only moved a single aisle (skipping chips and soda) into cleaning supplies when he made another request – "Dad I want some coconut shampoo."

I would have been less shocked if he asked for condoms. They are one aisle away. He could pick ribbed, lubricated, anything. I would look at him strange, laugh, and then move to get the broccoli for dinner. To coconut shampoo, I have no response. It is like the duck had an otter in the tub with him.

My simple response, "Really? Coconut?" Let's be plain, as creatures go, 12-year-old boys smell. They do not like to shower, or bathe. Getting into a car with a 12-year-old boy, who has opted out of a bathing ritual for days, is a rare indelicacy. The only surpassing odor would be a standard cheese tray in a French restaurant, and precisely why I do not eat cheese in French restaurants. When they do clean, they do not like soap. I threaten my children with loss of significant privileges to get them to bathe (even more so to get them to use soap). Yet, he stood before me begging for soap.

This is a dilemma. I can either let my son go the way of Carmen Miranda or try to toughen him up with the Lava Soap and Old Spice. If you think about it, what says you're a man more than washing with pieces of ground up pumice? Granted, this also causes horrible problems with your skin, but you have to sacrifice something for manliness.

Having given in to coconut shampoo, I am further amazed to find there are no fewer than 15 different brands. At that point, I did the only thing an "in-charge" father could do – I told him to pick one out while I got the vegetables. I ambled around the corner, cart in tow, leaving my doe-eyed preteen to rummage through the complexity that is shampoo in America.

Fifteen minutes, four stalks of broccoli, eight bananas, twelve apples, and various berries later I found my son staring at the condom aisle. Finally, I thought, a question I am prepared for; but, it never came. Instead, he looked at me again and announced he wanted body spray to go with his shampoo. At this point, there was no reason to fight deodorant, especially given his current mental state. I brushed my potential condom questions and answers aside, and we went to the checkout stand. He had his Pop-Tarts, his

Cowabunga Coconut Shampoo, and Axe body spray (it must be the commercials). We paid, carefully bagged his treasures, and walked out.

It is a cliché to say that a 12-year-old boy has one foot in our world and one in another, but it is true. He has a child's sweet-tooth, a teenager's awkwardness toward grooming, and the desire to take the next step forward into manhood. It is a time when he does not realize what he is struggling so hard to lose and just how precious these few moments of amazement he has left.

We got home; he unloaded the car, and he showered. My son used his new shampoo and pulled out the body spray. To say that the cloud he created was visible is not a gross exaggeration. On a positive note, I was able to cancel the exterminator for a month. In sufficient quantities, I believe that the average teenage body spray is more potent than insect poison. We left the Pop-Tarts for the next morning (there is no sense in overdoing the party).

I put the groceries away and sat down to read for a little while. That is when it came, "Dad, smell my armpits." I have yet to validate, but I am guessing he had just seen one of the Axe Instinct commercials. "Come on Dad, smell." I am the father, and the requirement to smell armpits falls into my domain. I just wanted to avoid the hair. The scent of coconut should be on the suntanned bodies of beautiful women – nothing else. In the end, yes, I smelled his armpit.

The body spray is better than the standard scent of a 12-year-old. And the smile he wore was indescribable. Perhaps I should consider a switch to Axe – it made him unbelievably happy, so there is something to be said about those commercials.

PICKING LOCKS

Having children is humbling. Humbling, not in the sense of awe you have at the birth of a child (truth be known, in men awe is often replaced by paralyzing fear); rather, humbling from the fact that all of your perceived strategies for being a good parent go right out the window most of the time.

♋

I wish I could say that I am a patient father. In the realm of TV dad example, I fall somewhere in between Al Bundy and Heathcliff Huxtable. I think there is a fair bit of the dad from the "Wonder Years" thrown in as well. Each time I find a sense of calm, my youngest son (he is ten) has a knack for finding the one thing that turns me into a blithering idiot.

I have to lock the doors in my house, and I am not talking about the front door. I mean the interior doors to my bedroom, my bedroom closet, my office, the laundry room, and the snack closet. This is done in a vain attempt to keep my youngest son from getting bored and exploring these areas with the abandon of a Spanish Conquistador pillaging the new world in search of gold.

When I do not lock my doors, I come home to a kitchen table filled with pieces of an old computer (one that I was saving) arranged like they have just been removed from an Ikea flat-pack.

To prevent these treasure hunts, I installed keyed doorknobs on many interior doors. This, of course, means that I now need to remember where I keep the keys. Moreover, whenever I really need to get into one of these rooms I have inevitably misplaced the keys. This is generally a short-lived frustration as he has become very good at figuring out where we hide the keys and he will generally run and get them for me.

My youngest son fancies himself quite a rogue, and thinks the whole concept of lock-picking is really neat. I have not had the heart to tell him that finding the hiding place of the keys is not the same as picking the lock. It is, instead, just another way to humble his father.

While there are many fallacies in my plan to lock myself into some sense of order – a major issue is that I keep all of the keys on a single ring. There has been many a stressful afternoon looking for all of the keys to my life as it were (at least until my son gets home from school and tells me where I last hid them).

One Saturday, I was having a particularly

difficult time finding the keys. In this case, I distinctly remember using them to unlock my office door a few hours earlier. I could have sworn I left them on the hall table. The problem with this particular loss was that many of the necessities of my life were interned on the other side of the door. After an hour of looking in every conceivable place, and even inconceivable places, like the refrigerator (long story), I went to see my son.

When faced with crisis I did what any reasonable parent would. First, I threatened him with many years of torture if he did not produce the keys. When that did not work, I resorted to bribery – $20 for any child that can produce the keys. After all else failed, I sat him down and told him that he had full amnesty if he could just explain to me what happened to the keys. Oddly enough, the third approach worked. He calmly explained that he found the keys in the hall and he placed them on the desk in my office and closed the door.

There are moments when blood rushes to your head and you must find the strength to hold your calm and honor the deal you just made. To be sure it was a Faustian moment for me. I sucked down the chaos, said thank you, sent him away, and tried to figure out my next step. The way I looked at it, I had a few choices: I could try to pick the lock, I could cut a hole in the door completely around the knob, or I could call a locksmith. Given that this is 10 p.m. on a Saturday evening, the locksmith idea was immediately disqualified. Further, men have enough trouble asking for directions (hence we now have GPS in cars), I could never bring myself to swallow this defeat. The angry portion of me wanted to immediately saw the hole in the door (the primal urge to destroy). The inquisitive portion of me, however, won out and I opted to pick the lock.

When you do a Google search on lock-picking you would be surprised how many things come up. First off, you need a bobby pin. I do not wear bobby pins. Unfortunately, neither does my wife. It turns out that you cannot crudely fashion a paper clip into a bobby pin shape and make it work. Also you need a tool that looks something like a dentist pick (something we all have at home). As I paced the hall, the angry side was starting to win – I could barely keep the thought of the reciprocating saw out of my mind. I do happen to have one of those at home.

One of the more interesting options for trying to pick a lock is to make a bump key. The mere fact that any 10-year-old can make one of these things and use it to open any door is a fairly disconcerting fact and speaks volumes to the perception of security we have when the reality is screaming insecurity.

In every man's life there is that toolbox – the one that sits in the corner of the garage with all of the emergency tools. Mine happens to be yellow. It contains a haphazard collection of implements – a hammer, level, dry-wall anchors, mismatched drill-bits, and other less recognizable novelties. I am not organized. As such, my toolbox is not organized. Making a bump key involves a key that fits the door and a metal file. I own a file, it is not at home. It is in another (less organized toolbox) in a storage facility that is closed after 9 p.m. on Saturdays. The bump key was out.

Having children is humbling. Staring at the reciprocating saw, all I could think is that I have been beaten by the machinations of a 10-year-old, 83 pound, blond ball of fury. That is when a miracle happened. I went to replace the scattered contents of my little yellow toolbox and lying at the bottom was a simple, rusty hacksaw blade with a rubber handle. I look at a hacksaw as the catch all tool (a more violent duct-tape). If you have a problem, metal or wood, a hacksaw can generally cut through it (at which point you can quietly throw it away and forget that it ever existed).

My calculations earlier in the evening had failed to reveal a fourth option that that wisdom of the hacksaw now revealed. I could save the door, and simply remove the doorknob. For the record, it is never as easy to saw through metal as you would think. It can be especially difficult to saw through a piece of metal that is round, thereby making it hard for the saw to grip. This did not occur to me when I approached the doorknob brandishing the saw like Conan going into battle. During the first 30 minutes of sawing through the doorknob I lost some will and grabbed a folding chair out of the garage. I did, however, get a spectator. My youngest sat down right next to me. He was fascinated with my "lock-picking" technique, as he put it. He sat there and smiled at me for the next 45 minutes as I slowly managed to move the saw through the metal. By the time the knob fell to the floor he had me laughing. When I finally grabbed the vice-grips to turn the internal workings of the lock, he was beaming. When we opened the door (and retrieved the keys) – I was his hero for the night.

I have not had the heart to tell him that this is not picking a lock either. For now, I will just be cool. In the eyes of your child that will pass eventually, you have to take the victories when you can.

PATCHES

Lunacy is not reserved to the current generation. Every time my children do something that makes me question their need to exist, I try to remember that I was not radically better at their age. I know from experience the devastation a 12-year-old mind can cause (very often to yourself). Lurking deep in the heart of every 12-year-old boy is a scientist. There is a great adventurer who seeks to discover everything about his amazing world. Why does the sun rise? Why does lightning strike? How do planes fly? What actually happens to aerosol cans if you puncture them?

♋

While most of those questions require true research, the last only requires opportunity and motivation. Ideally, you need an empty house with mom and dad at work, two friends coming over, and a can with a warning that reads, "Contents under pressure – may explode if punctured."

The word "explode" holds a special meaning for a 12-year-old boy. It lacks the mature connotations of death and danger. Rather, to a young boy, "explode" is exciting and adventurous. In the binary preteen mind, explosions mean power. This one particular day I recall from my youth, my friends (Chris and Ryan) were passengers along for the ride. In a very real way, I was mad with pleasure. But, I needed help; so, with my partners in terrorism, I set out to rule to world (or at least my block).

First, I needed an instrument of destruction. It had to be something just right. I had to be able to harness and direct the force onto the can. A metal stake? Too short. A broom handle? Too weak. With distracted and frenzied thought, it came to me. Chris's father was installing a new chain-link fence. We could use a hollow piece of fence pipe. It made perfect sense – a long, hollow barrel for the most powerful weapon ever created. All we needed, now, was ammunition. It took only a few moments of digging in our garages, and project "D-Day" was underway. Thinking back now, the "D" stands for dumb.

Back then we were proud soldiers, holding our head's high in our mission. We triumphantly marched into the vacant lot behind Ryan's house and (in that dusty corner of our neighborhood) – we began. First, I set up a paint can. The angle had to be just right. Then we had to determine who would be the first to drive home the piston and release the awesome explosive power. As I was the fearless leader of our crew, the answer was obvious – Ryan would do it.

Chris and I stood, breathless, eyes focused on Ryan. It seemed in slow motion. He raised the pipe up above his head and with a single thrust...

There are few times in life when reality completely fulfills your expectations, a time when you feel truly free and at one with nature. This was one of those moments.

A perfect mushroom cloud of sparkling white paint burst from the top of the barrel, floating down softly in a shimmering cloud – gently reflecting the sunlight. It was akin to a religious experience. I could only think that this is what the Manhattan project scientists must have felt when they finally succeeded. No one could stop us now. With delusions of grandeur in our head, we moved forward.

There are very few afternoons in memory that rival the pure pleasure of that one – three friends playing together, laughing, and working towards a common goal. All day long we fired our new toy, sending eruption after eruption of multicolored enamel into the stratosphere. As the sun sank, our ammunition waned, and Chris and Ryan retreated (gloriously covered in paint) to their homes. Turning to make my way back home, I saw it. A single, pristine can lay in the middle of the lot. This was the last can, and it was mine. My hands reached greedily forward and positioned the shell. The label read, "Antiseptic Spray." These are words I will never forget.

Once again, I placed the can down on the

firing pad. I stood as a lone warrior against his foe. Instead of simply stabbing the can, I felt it would be better to step back and thrust the pole like a javelin at my target. Taking Spartan-like aim, I let my make-shift spear fly. In an instant, the air was split with a thunderous crack. It must have been a sight to behold. Unfortunately, I could not see it. The last thing I saw (for quite a while) was the fast moving cloud of antiseptic hitting me square in the eyes.

To a 12-year-old mind (maybe to the male species in general), explosives are cool; and, every "dangerous" expedition of a young boy triumphantly (or pathetically) ends up in battle wounds. I wore patches over both eyes for two-weeks. For the record, one eye-patch is pirate-cool – two eye-patches is pathetic. For two weeks I got to sit in darkness. I missed the Fourth of July fireworks the following weekend. The worst part was that I had to miss my GI Joe cartoons. However, I did manage to sneak a peek or two (when mom and dad were not looking).

FILL THE PAGE

What no one ever told me about being a parent was the pain it would cause. All the books talk about the joy of children. Some even talk about the chaos your life becomes, and the natural high you get from sleep deprivation. But what you do not hear about, from my recollection, is the emotional pain. It starts as a dull ache the day you first meet your son, and becomes almost crippling as the years move him closer to adulthood. It is the pain that comes from the realization that wonderful and frustrating things he brings into your life every day are only temporary – that, eventually, he has to walk on his own.

♋

What you realize, all too quickly, is that you are nowhere near as good as you want to be at being a parent. I will take it a step further – one of the things I am coming to realize is that I am horrible. Do not get me wrong, I love my children, but there is never a day when I feel like I do anything particularly right. I have to imagine (or at least hope) that this is a universal state.

As my children age, and their interests diverge from my own, I find myself looking for ways to be around them. A few weeks ago, it was a haircut. I had one scheduled, and I dragged my oldest along. This is, admittedly, a mundane activity; but there are points when any time is good time. At least, we could talk during the ride. Small activities can sometimes provide the best memories. For instance, on his twelfth birthday, I taught him to use the grill. This was my best attempt at a testosterone-laden rite of passage. There are few things better in life than fire and meat. Fifteen minutes into that afternoon, he was standing at the grill, sweating, and singing along to the Goo Goo Dolls – his iPod headphones glued in his ears. He was listening to a song called "Still Your Song." Listening to it a few days later, I came across a line that stuck in my head – "I fill the page with my beliefs, it's all I have to keep. Tear it up and start again."

I characterize being a parent in just that way. You fill your children with everything. You give them your passion, your fear, your values, everything. At first, these may simply begin as the knee-jerk reactions of your culture, but, either consciously or subconsciously, we draw deeper and deeper lines in the pages that mark their life. My beliefs have changed over the years. I have had to tear up a lot of pages and start over. When it comes to your children, all you can hope

is that the lessons that you write into their being translates into a happy life, and that they do not have to tear up too much.

Not all days are about barbecue grills and musical lyrics aside. Some days, it is a more mundane activity that brings us together. Today, it was a trip to the stylist. I am often busy – that day was no different. By the time we reached the salon, I was ten minutes late and flustered. Palo Alto is trendy, but in a muted fashion. The downtown area is a subdued hamlet of little specialty shops. The few chain stores have to be trendy, and quietly blend in. We hurried into the salon; and my son hopped right on one of the computers (they have them reserved for clientele) to play around and I took my place in the shampoo chair.

Twenty minutes later, having forgotten about the mad rush to get to the salon, my son walked out of the backroom and to my chair. My stylist, Steve, and I were talking about his impending trip to New York (doing hair for fashion week) when my son sat in the chair next to me. He did not say anything, he just sat and listened. This is a new development, he observes me in conversations – I would like to say listen instead of observe; but he is a teenager, he never listens. It is like he is trying to figure out how to be an adult by watching. What he will likely figure out at some point in his life is that the older I get, the more of a child I become.

Not long after sitting down, he asks if he can go to Starbucks. My son has recently started to lust after Starbucks (at least it is coffee and not girls). In another one of those "do what I say" imperfect parent moments, I am trying to keep him from my coffee habit. Currently, we have settled on the green tea Frappuccino as an alternative. If you think about it, that is the perfect Palo Alto coffee substitute. It is an ideal yippee drink (this is a yuppie who wants to act like a hippie).

I pulled a ten dollar bill out of my pocket and handed it over. I think he loves the Starbucks concept for two reasons. First, he gets a treat. Second, he gets a little independence. It is only two stores down, but to him it may as well have been a different world. The older he gets, the more he likes doing things on his own. For me, of course, it is the opposite. The older he gets, the more I want him to do things with me.

Steve and I dropped back into casual conversation, and again, I let life's worries fade into the background. Flights, haircuts, long car trips – these are times when I find I can relax the most. I actually let go. Finding peace in a small, seemingly insignificant moment is something I hope my children inherit from me. My coffee habit is something I hope they do not.

After about 20 minutes my oldest came back, drink in hand. This is when the battle begins. In the history of fathers and sons, there can be no longer-running battle than that of the change. His job is to keep the change from the purchase and squirrel it away. Money is, in many respects, independence. My job is to get what is left of the money back (to retain a little control). I somehow doubt he ever gives me back all the change; and, truth be known, I am often fine with him keeping the few dollars. Nonetheless, the father and son battle handbook clearly states that we have a conversation about the change.

Playing my part, I ask. I am expecting his reply to be that there is not much, or that he bought a cookie with it, or an open hand with a few quarters. I did not expect what he said. "I do not have any, I gave it to the lady," he said, "She was sitting on the sidewalk, and looked like she needed it." I asked him if she asked him for anything, he said no, she just seemed like she could use it.

Your memory gets better as a parent, not worse. You find that you remember, sometimes in a melancholy way, things that are beautiful. That was one of those moments that will always stick with me. A simple five dollars means nothing to me. To her, the money (and the gesture from a child) was possibly the best thing that happened to her in a long time. Sometimes the kindness and charity of the world is all we have to hold on to.

Maybe it is simply the beauty of childhood, and a sense of fair-play, that made him give her the money. I am hoping that it is something more. Maybe I filled a page for him that speaks of charity and dignity of a person. He definitely filled a page for me. That one I will not tear up. That one is worth keeping.

WE DO NOT TAKE CORN CHIPS
TO THE BATHROOM

The complexity of children will forever be a mystery to me. I would like to believe that I was a simpler child – not the kind of boy that would shatter the Arcadia window with a pellet gun while trying to shoot a target blind-folded. I know I was no better or worse than any child; but, living an illusion is sometimes comforting.

♋

What amazes me are the seemingly logical things we (parents) take for granted, and that they (children) do not fathom. I am convinced they have secret meetings to plan for our devolution into insanity. Case in point is the many recent hours I spent looking for a large glass bowl full of corn chips (Scoops to be exact). I had made a particularly nice dip for a party the prior evening and I wanted some left-overs. After scouring the kitchen, the bedrooms, and the garage, I relented and asked my youngest son.

In my house, my youngest is the oracle of Delphi. He knows more about what is happening in my life than I do. His interest in understanding all activities within our house is reminiscent of the stereotypical prison boss. Nothing is removed, lost, stolen, eaten, broken, or so forth without his direct knowledge. At times, things seem to require his permission. Given his proclivity for mischief, there are times that I think he is more poltergeist than human. On this afternoon, I found him, playing in the garage. I asked about the chips, he looked at me with his oracle-like stare and said "They are in the bathroom." It turns out his brother left them there. The bathroom, for reasons that escape me as an adult, seems to be the catch-all room for my children.

My house, very often, exists in a state of controlled chaos. With two boys, two dogs, two cats, and two adults in 1700 square feet on three levels – there is stress. To alleviate stress, there are rules; and, in some cases, less freedom.

I had not explicitly created a rule that prohibited corn chips from the bathroom. Not taking food to the bathroom always seemed to be a sort of given, an in-born logic if you will. I had thought this would be like swimming. Most animals can swim at birth – dogs, cats, horses, etc. Primates, on the other hand, cannot. It has to do (so I am told) with higher level thinking skills. We have enough common sense to fear water – so we panic and drown. As bad as that sounds, there is beauty in the fact that we can overcome fear and act on desire as opposed to just instinct (even when it is counterproductive to common sense). It is beautiful in the case of swimming, less so with food and the bathroom. At no point did I expect to find corn chips in the bathroom. I found them carefully placed behind the door, my oldest nowhere to be seen.

This was upsetting on two levels. First, Scoops are, perhaps, the perfect chip. They are an edible spoon for dip, and something that should be called out as an additional required food group. Once brought into the bathroom, however, they are then considered tainted and must be discarded. Second, and more importantly, I now had to eat dip with a non-edible spoon.

To a degree, I understand the chaos. They are not growing up the way I did. When I was a kid I used to disappear for the entire day. I would get up in the morning, have breakfast, and leave. I might come home for lunch, I might not. I would roam the neighborhoods, go see friends, or find a hideout in the desert. I lived in Las Vegas for a number of years. It is where I had my first taste of freedom. I remember at one point my friends and I built a fort in a creosote bush in the desert. One of the guys had a bunch of old Playboy magazines he stole from his older brother. We hid them there; we were rebels with no thought beyond that day.

That is the most beautiful thing about being a child, I think. They do not think about tomorrow, except to dream of the time when their "real life will start." When you are young, everything is about the moment. You can celebrate the sunrise, weep at the sunset, and five minutes more to play is truly an eternity. I ache with the realization that the world I make for my boys is not the same world I knew. The mischievous mind-set is the same, but circumstances are very different. Perhaps it is better – I would hope – but I am not sure. There are so many rules to life; and it gets worse as we age. Where possible, I try to give them freedom. But taking your Game Boy and snacks to the bathroom is odd. The bathroom is not a place you need to multi-task, especially with food. There is now a strict no corn chips in the bathroom rule.

I caught them dancing once – they were playing a video game. My oldest was dancing with the controllers in the kitchen, and my youngest was standing on the kitchen table mimicking his every move. I did not get mad (generally out of my character); instead, I found patience and laughed. I quit being a religious man many years ago, but I do pray. My prayer that night was about being patient enough to allow them to have more fun. It was a prayer for their innocence. That will, of course, require fewer rules on my part. I have never been good at them anyways. However, the corn chip rule stays in place – we have to have some limits.

TIME TO MEASURE UP

Pubic hair!
I said it. It's on the table. If you go through all the volumes of texts known to exist, I would speculate that you would find less than ten (and I am being generous) that begin with the phrase pubic hair. In fact, I would suspect that any creative writing journal, textbook, or blog you can think of would caution against discussing this as a primary topic. As a father, I have come to think differently. While I cannot claim any medical pedigree, I would suspect the genetic makeup of the hair is equivalent across the body. Maybe it is simply the length and grooming that differentiates one from another? If you think about it, pubic hair faces geographic discrimination, like living in Alabama.

☍

You might ask, with all of the material available, why choose this particular topic? The answer is as simple as gravity; I have sons. As the father, biological changes in boys often falls to me for discussion. At this point, a more responsible writer would look for analogies and clever symbolism to maintain some level of dignity or decorum. However, since we started in an abnormal fashion, there is little point in attempting a polite facade. With that sentiment in mind, let me just state that my youngest is both better endowed and much better covered than his older brother.

Before moving any further, for sake of legal defense, let me say that I do not go out of my way to make these observations. Instead, my boys go out of their way to provide me with material. They observe everything. And (with the jubilance only a child can muster) they wake you early on a Sunday morning, naked, with the representative parts at eye level. This is done so you can get the exact count from their prepubescent garden. There is no parenting book that explains this happening. It never occurred to me that this would ever be the first image burned into my cornea on a warm Sunday morning.

I do not recall much joy in puberty or being enamored of the changes. Conversely, both of my boys are awestruck by this state of being. They have hair. This is a milestone. I am their guide through life's amusement park, at present, so their triumphs are mine. And, on a very surreal note, given my current follicular state, we have bonded. Because, as my oldest stated at one point, "Dad, you are in puberty as well." Again, I do not remember reading this section in the parent manual.

With respect to books on parenting, you have What to Expect When You're Expecting, and even The Girlfriends' Guide to Pregnancy (written by an ex-Playboy Playmate, I bought this solely for the articles). There is not, however, The Fathers Guide to Hair, Girth, and Rude Awakenings. When they discover the other joy of puberty, I may leave that discussion to their mother. The timing will become apparent either through the laundry or the sudden extension and frequency of mid-day showers. She is likely to notice first. History being a guide, I am likely to be shuffled into the bedroom for that discussion.

While walking the dogs together last weekend, my oldest looked at me and asked, "Dad, why does my brother have more hair than I do? Is something wrong with me?" Sometimes I think, compared to children, men are cowards. Children ask the hard questions and we have to choose how to respond. Sometimes we choose not to respond – out of fear.

Thinking about it, however, it is fear (the fear of being different) that caused my son to ask. Puberty is not really joyful. He knows he is growing and changing and that is exciting, but he is scared (as is his brother). All they want to know is that they are not different, that they are following the expected path. I guess as a child they follow the yellow brick road without a choice, they need the scarecrow (brain or not) to help them skip along.

On that walk, I explained to my son that he was fine. That we all change differently, and that I was proud of him for getting bigger and for having the courage to ask. Something tells me that, as a father, this topic – the topic of, "How am I developing in life, am I ok?" – is something he and I, and his brother and I, will revisit for years, maybe decades, to come. I can't say where my life will lead tomorrow – years ago I decided that was a futile activity. As a father it is time to measure up and find my courage. Pubic hair happens, and there is nothing you can do about it.

WAITING FOR MY REAL LIFE

There is an innate desire in the human spirit that looks to carve out a place of its very own, a retreat of sorts. For years they will seem to be content strapped to your chest, or riding on your shoulders in a crowd at the parade. Then, before you know it, they are creating forts from pillows and blankets in the living room. The fort is the first step to finding a personal sanctuary – a very important one.

☞

Looking back now, with the eyes of a father, those days of forts and special treasures hold a different meaning. As an adult I am not sure I am yet to find a place as special as the ones made of bed sheet walls from the youth. Friday evenings were often filled with requests to move kitchen chairs, and the couch, and to pull books off the shelf to create the makeshift world from my sons' imagination. It is as if they are preparing to build a world of their own. The fort is a simple, symbolic first step.

Those evenings of fort building remind me of one of my favorite songs. It is titled "Waiting for My Real Life to Begin," by Colin Hay. For any child of the 80s, he is better known as the lead singer from Men at Work. While I loved his music growing up, it is better now with a few additional decades in his voice.

When my boys were little, fort building was often a Friday activity. For many years, I traveled for work, when my sons were young. Truth be known, I continue to travel now that they are older. Because of this, Fridays and weekends are filled with travel penance activities. In my house, forts were an activity of choice, and gifts from abroad were the desired currency. Realistically speaking, gifts (I think) were a tradition started by parents to make themselves feel better about being gone. Before children, traveling for work appears glamorous. Whether it is Paris or Des Moines, there is an allure to living on the road. It may seem odd to place Paris and Des Moines in the same sentence, but having been to both over the years (in both good and bad weather), Des Moines is highly under-rated (Paris is never overrated). Des Moines aside, for the wayward father gifts are travel penance.

Having established the importance of gifts, at least for the wanderlust stricken father, we need to also establish that I am particular. Wandering through an airport, there is no shortage of plastic toys and cheap jewelry. These are a poor substitute for any kind of real thought. Buying a necklace in duty free on a transatlantic flight, for instance, does not count as Christmas shopping. The value in a gift (to me) is not the cost; rather, it is the value the recipient places on it. To that end, the last day, or few hours, of my trips are sometimes spent trying to think of something of value.

With my boys, the key is either sugar or toys. From Amsterdam, it was chocolate. From London, a scale model of a Mini Cooper. Having two boys, you try to ensure balance. What you buy for one, you often buy for the other. This distribution of wealth makes sense to the adult mind; it does not always translate equally in the world of children. For example, when I bring toys home, my oldest takes the toys, plays with them, breaks them and then searches for his brother's toy to break.

Because of this trend, my youngest is quite protective of his things. I have had to break up more than one physical altercation over the sum total of $8.49, plus tax. To prevent the incipient looting of his treasures, my youngest has started hiding things. He hides his things, my things, my wife's things – he hides everything he can to keep them out of his brother's "evil hands."

Last weekend I was cleaning the garage. As our townhouse does not have a yard or a basement, the garage has become – and I fear will forever remain – the boys' playground. There is a little crawl space at the back of our garage. It is the ultimate fort (sans the blanket walls). I have forbidden the boys from playing in there. It is where we store the fragile Christmas decorations, and other things I would prefer to remain whole. As this area is forbidden, they are in there constantly. They often rearrange the boxes to cover their tracks and remember to turn off the light. Still, the tell-tale sign of Nerf gun darts is a dead giveaway.

This "fort" is a genuine crawlspace; I have to be on my hands and knees to move around. Kneeling on a hard, concrete floor (at this point in my life) is medieval. To mitigate the pain, I placed a bunch of spare carpet in the crawl space. This had the desired effect of making it easier to move around. This also had the undesired effect of making it all the more cozy for my pre-teen interlopers. Crawling into their world, the boxes of Christmas decorations were stacked into a makeshift castle wall. Smiling, I started to rearrange them back into place. When I moved the third box, something fell off the stack and hit me in the head. After a momentary bout of cursing and a spot check for blood, I looked around, trying to determine the offending item. It was my youngest son's treasure box (one of his favorite hiding places).

He likes boxes. For some reason, the concept of containers fascinates him. This one was made by his grandfather. It has a slide lid, and a drawer pull off of a kitchen cabinet to open and close. This box is his most prized possession. Picking it up from the carpet, I slid the top open. The inventory was quite simple, Bakugan (a toy hidden from his brother), some "crystal rocks" (given to him by his grandfather), a silver coin (I bought him at the Kennedy Space Center), and a series of golden quarters. He had been collecting the quarters for years. This was everything of value in his world.

Laughing, I replaced the lid and slid the box back to the top of the pile. Over the years, throughout my travels, I have spent time toiling over the perfect gift. His box taught me something of perfection, of desire. The things in his box were not possessions to him, they were happy memories. Those were the moments when people paid attention to the special human being he is. I guess, like the fort, they were moments when he could define (could see) his world, for himself. Clarity of vision can never be underestimated, at any age. Again, to quote Colin (and my favorite song), "On a clear day I can see, see for a long way."

BOYS OF A CERTAIN AGE

The concept of bunny-hopping a bicycle is odd. If you are unfamiliar, a "bunny hop" is when, while riding a bike, the rider thrusts his body upward. He pulls on the handlebars, and then jerks his feet in and up.

♋

When executed successfully, the bike hops off the ground with the rider still attached. When executed unsuccessfully, the rider slips off the pedals and the top bar of the bike frame delivers a particularly painful blow to a particularly delicate portion of the anatomy. This outcome is actually more likely than the successful attempt when wearing wet sneakers.

The bike, by its very design, was meant to reside firmly affixed to the surface of the Earth. Tires need more friction than that found in-flight to be useful. As children care nothing for the laws of physics and good sense, the bunny hop is popular with the pre-teen crowd. Also, if I remember correctly, it was quite attractive to the 10- to 12-year-old girl demographic when I was young.

Realistically speaking, men do nothing if it does not somehow make them at least a little more appealing to the opposite sex – 12-year-olds are no different (even if they do not realize it). The other day, I was teaching my oldest son this most important bicycle trick. He is twelve.

For many reasons, twelve is a seminal moment in a young man's life. He still plays with Legos and blocks, but in the back of his mind he is starting to look at girls and realize that blocks, in many cases, are far less interesting than curves. It is the time (if I remember correctly) in which you feel the most invincible.

I envy the 12-year-old mind in so many ways. He sings just to hear the resonance of his voice, he draws because it makes him happy, and he experiments with everything around him. I love that joy, and I do not want to do anything to discourage his attitude; however, since a 12-year-old does not know that the world can hurt you, sometimes a bunny-hopping lesson results in the negative, slippery-shoe outcome and a lesson in reality. The ultimate lesson – do not be overly careless, give a little deference to the nature of the physical world, or you can get hurt. In fact I would call this a rule instead of a lesson. A universal constant we all come to realize, and one that life is generally ready to teach.

One of the best things about being a father is reliving all of your own lunacy. A close second is witnessing the evolution of ever sillier ideas over the generations. I cannot speak for a girl, but when it comes to boys, there is no shortage of stupidity for the sake of a little adrenalin.

Personally, I have never taken stock in most rules. Do not get me wrong, I tend to follow the rules of polite society. I am not an anarchist – more a contrarian. In many ways my children are the same, they come by it naturally. That (among many other things) is really my fault. Having said that, it never ceases to amaze me how the machinations of the pre-teen mind seek to wreak havoc on the laws of both physics and sanity.

A 12-year-old seems to have the innate desire to test the limits of your world. There are those times when you might jump off the roof of a house with nothing more than an umbrella. It works in the cartoons, so of course it must work in real life. Then there are those times when you take your boogie board out of the closet and surf down the stairs. Given that my home has two landings from upstairs to downstairs, it is a tricky task to successfully navigate from level to level. In reality I am not as concerned from a safety perspective as I am from a quality perspective.

The level of math required to map the angles down the stairs, off the wall, across both landings and then safely into the living room is well beyond his sixth grade capabilities. Anything worth doing is worth doing right. Until he can do the math, I am officially prohibiting stair surfing.

The umbrella trick is something (you would think) that I do not need to make a rule about – this can immediately follow "No corn-chips in the bathroom." It is only logical that this is a bad idea. Unfortunately, with 12-year-old boys, there is little logic, and God knows it never stopped me.

A TRIP TO DOLLYWOOD MAY BE IN ORDER

Boys are rough-and-tumble. Sons, in my experience, should not be coddled. To the contrary, they function best when they have bumps and bruises from wrestling with their brother or the family dog. Cleanliness, decorum, and polite society are not only lost on a proper boy, they never occur to him. Boys, in short, have little touch with reality until much later in life. The careful reader may notice that I did not specify an age. There are dear friends of mine (women) who would state that this moment of epiphany never arrives for most men. In deference to that widespread opinion, I will defer any discussion on age of maturity. Boys are a different breed. My youngest son, is all boy. The idea of kissing a girl is repulsive to him. Pink is the color of the wedding gown worn by Satan's bride, and Vin Diesel is his idol.

I am lying. That does not describe my younger son. It is a more apt description of my older. My youngest kissed his first girl (not his mother) in second grade. Her name was Madison, and I hear about her constantly. He collects rocks, and adores rose quartz, and his favorite movie is *Titanic.*

Every so often, he and his mother sit down and watch with rapt intensity as Jack and Rose hurtle towards their predestined conclusion. He is never still for anything, but he is still for that movie. Watching him view that film always amazes me. Do not get me wrong, I like the movie. I respect the cinematic achievement and enjoy the drama. I would not, however, place it in the annual viewing category the way the Sound of Music was in my home growing up. Nonetheless, my youngest loves the movie *Titanic*; and, this is how I found myself in Knoxville, Tennessee. Specifically, this is how I found myself in Pigeon Forge, Tennessee.

In the summer of 2011 my family decided it was time for the children to see the country. To that end, we loaded up our car and embarked on a seven week, 7,000 mile Summer of Love tour. There were of course the obligatory stops at national parks, big cities, and Pigeon Forge, Tennessee. Until recently, the greater Pigeon Forge / Gatlinburg metro area's main claim to fame was Dolly Parton. She was born there, and that is where she opened Dollywood. If you have never been to Pigeon Forge, it is hard to describe. It is similar to the Wisconsin Dells, without the water, but with its own Ripley's Believe It or Not museum. In the days of Dolly's childhood, I would suspect that Pigeon Forge was a sleepy town on the river, a place nestled in the Smoky Mountains where Tom Sawyer would settle. Now, it is where carnies go to retire. Until recently, this would not have been on my bucket list (or really any list that I may pen), but in April of 2010, Pigeon Forge became home to the Titanic Museum. So, we ended up in Pigeon Forge.

The Titanic museum is a full scale replica of the first one-third of the ship. The people working at the museum are dressed in period costume and they attempt period accents (mostly British). When you enter the museum, you find out that the price of admission does not include the automated audio tour gadget. For an extra $10 (per person) you can have the full Titanic experience. Given my proclivity for gadgets, $40 total seemed a small price to pay to ensure that my personal visit to the Titanic was as geeky as possible – as if showing up in the first place was not geeky enough.

The museum separates in to rooms that are replicas of the ship on the night it sailed. You move from servant's quarters, through first class berths, into the engine room, the ballroom, and so on. They even have a room with a wall of ice representing the iceberg (that you can touch) and 28 degree salt water in troughs so you can place your arm in the water and feel what that water temperature felt like to passengers.

In each room, you type the number (or numbers) on the wall into your audio tour and receive a detailed story about both the ship and the people. When you start the tour, you get a sheet of paper with a brief biography of one of the passengers. You get to learn about that person's experiences along the way, and find out at the end if they survived. This one aspect makes the tour very personal.

My youngest did not pay any attention to his person. He bounced with excitement from room to room, looking at the "treasures" raised from the bottom of the sea. For him, this was an adventure.

I admit I softened my stance as we went along. The artifacts were genuine, the displays impeccable, and the stories mesmerizing. I am getting older, and a little softening is to be expected; but, to my surprise, my oldest (Vin Diesel attitude stowed away) softened as well. He ran ahead in each room, but he ran back to show me what he found. In one room he found, and loved, the dog kennel where passenger's pets traveled. He told me the story he read on the wall that described how many pets managed to escape. He took a liking to the bone china in the first-class dining area. Sometimes we found, and liked, the same things. Sometimes we did not – I did not care about the specific dimensions of the dog kennels or how many ferrets were on board; but, we both got lost in the moment together. For the record, he even beat me in a contest to see who could hold their arm in the frigid water the longest. I like to think I let him win (even getting older I cannot give up all male posturing).

In the end, my oldest son's person died, he

was a crewman on the ship. He shoveled coal. My person died as well, he was a wealthy industrialist (a billionaire by today's standards). It was a stunning dichotomy. By all accounts, both were good, charitable men from different worlds, lost in a moment together.

My son was visibly disappointed when we got to the memorial wall at the end of the museum and he found his name on the wall of the deceased. I tickled him, got him to laugh, and he hugged me. There are teachable moments; and, there are moments when anything I could teach would be beyond his years. I wanted to tell him the story of the minister that I read on one of the plaques. He went into the water that night next to a teenage boy. They clung to debris waiting for a lifeboat to save them. The minister told the boy to accept God and prey. He then removed his life jacket and gave it to the boy. Minutes later, the minister slipped into the depths and died. The boy was saved soon afterward.

I wanted to tell him that death is ok, if you live for something (no matter how small). I do not know if that minister lived his life the way he did in his last moments, but in his last few moments he proved that he lived for something, and died honoring it. Nothing I would have said would have mattered at that point, the experience taught him everything he needed on that night. A smile and a hug worked wonders for him and miracles for me.

My preconceptions of the museum and the experience were wrong. I can now check Pigeon Forge and the Titanic museum off my bucket list, and do so with a smile. My oldest can as well, even though (like me) he did not realize that it needed to be on there.

Given the success of the night, I am thinking a trip to Dollywood may be in order. Maybe lightening could strike twice – having said that, as bucket list items go, I am not sure if I am brave enough to attempt it.

THOUGHTS OF FEDORAS AND
FANCY SHOES

M any mornings in my house start with a slamming door. The standard hollow core door found in most homes these days (at least those built in the last decade) are, at best, illusory guards of privacy. They seem little more than molded saw-dust, water, and glue pumped into one of ten standard molds. They are then primed, covered with a dull white sheen of paint and stacked in the local hardware warehouse. I would say store, but I have this fantasy that the old hardware store stocked significantly higher quality merchandise. This is likely a minor, deluded fantasy of my youth brought on by memories of wandering through aisles of intricate nuts, bolts, and tools with my father.

♋

The doors in my house are somewhat flimsy and very, very light. It is on the last point that I am most amazed. As light as these doors are, when my children (generally my youngest) decide to pull a sneak attack on the other (to say good morning) and runs away screaming from the newly awakened and enraged sibling, the fact he can slam these light doors with such reverberating force is a universal enigma.

That is how my Saturday mornings frequently begin – my youngest screaming (in perfect male soprano pitch), running down the hall, and slamming his door. This is quickly followed by the incipient thud of his older brother hitting the door with his fists in a vain, but spirited effort to gain entry and exact a measure of teenage justice (generally involving some form of "dead leg").

I normally intervene mid-tirade, pulling the injured soul away from the door and shuffling with him back to his room. It is at those moments when I wish I had incense burning and Gregorian chant albums queued up on a Clapper. Anything to help defuse the drama at that point is wonderful. This morning was no different. I quickly moved my oldest back to his room, turned on the Xbox and sat with him as he settled into a series of bloody raids on aliens on some distant planet.

I am adjusting to the thought that my son is now a teenager. I, of course, have the standard parent memories and the box of pictures to match. In a melancholy moment, I sometimes recall him as a toddler, sitting in a push car, and wearing a plastic, red colander on his head. More often, however, I am fascinated by the nuances of being a teenager and spend hours trying to figure out what makes him tick. That was what I was doing while watching him play his games. In a very real way, he relaxes when he plays, even at times when his younger brother has him physically shuddering with thoughts of revenge.

I let him play and went down to make breakfast. Being that this was his birthday weekend, I needed to make something interesting. Chocolate chip pancakes are a specialty. I make them thick (at least a quarter inch), and make sure they can break open with chocolate goodness like the cookies on the Nestle Toll House commercials. If there is one thing that will bring a teenage boy out of a Halo induced coma (at least in my house), it is chocolate in one of its many forms.

Once my oldest finished his breakfast, I told him to get dressed. We had errands to run. Any normal Saturday I would have spared him the scavenger hunt that is removing seemingly random items from the "honey-do" list. Today, however, one of the items was new clothes – some birthday clothes. For this, I needed his help.

Going to the mall with a teenager (even a preteen) is an interesting experience. It is a little bit like a battle. You (the parent) need to accomplish your mission leveraging the fewest resources possible. Your opponent (the child) is attempting to circumvent your mission by expanding its scope and consuming resources with abandon.

Do not get me wrong, I do not mind shopping. Quite to the contrary, I enjoy wandering around stores from time to time. Just the week prior, I had gone out to replace a pair of worn dress shoes. I learned long ago that good shoes and a good drywall guy are worth the money. Even so, we all have a budget. That particular Saturday, I took my advice (in a roundabout way) and tried on a pair of Italian leather, cap-toe dress shoes. Vanity got the better of me, overriding my common sense filters, and I spent my shoe budget many times over. While I was a little remorseful after the purchase, they fit like track shoes and I feel good when I wear them. This particular Saturday, however, was not about shoes; instead, I was clothes shopping for a soon-to-be teenager.

My local mall is likely similar to any one of thousands of clones across American suburbs – two levels, multiple corridors, a food court, and an endless supply of clothing stores. Shopping with a teenage boy (perhaps any teenager) is about being trendy. I remember owning a pair of parachute pants, back in my youth. The search for trendy is fine. What I find difficult, at least as I get older, is how to not look creepy while wandering through Abercrombie or the myriad other stores designed to cater to the preteen and teenage consumer.

He has not started looking, at least not overtly, at the teenage models on the posters. I, of course, attempt to not raise my eyes or quickly sweep by while trying to find clothing. As the models on the posters wear very little clothing, looking to them for guidance would be a waste anyways. Not long after arriving we settled into Aeropostale. This was good on two fronts. First, they were having a sale. Second, they had very few posters.

His goal for the day was to acquire a nice new pair of torn jeans. My goal was to ensure that he enjoyed himself, but also to make sure that he had a pair of nice, new unperforated jeans for more formal events (for a teenage boy, jeans are formal attire). If I have learned anything over the last few years about would-be teenagers, it is that sometimes negotiation is required to move the game in your favor. To that end, I picked out two pair of jeans – one pristine, and the other strategically torn, frayed, and partially faded. The latter, of course, were three times the price of the former. I can only speculate that it is the cost of the textile artist involved in creating the perfectly symmetrical frays on the upper right thigh. After going through multiple sizes, style discussions, and bargains, we finally settled our negotiations on two pair of jeans, a flannel shirt (a la Kurt Cobain), a thick belt, and two hoodies. The hoodies were buy one get one free. I took this as a silent victory, and a sign that in the overall battle of teenage and adult wills, I was victorious.

My oldest was happy – he had the store clerks (more teenage fashion poster models) remove the alarm tags from the clothing and wore one of his new outfits out of the store. It was at that point that he pulled out the birthday ice cream cone ploy. Even if I did not like ice-cream (which I do very much) this is impossible to resist. We wandered back toward the food court.

In recent years, he has developed a habit of becoming quiet and pensive when he wants something. This is in stark contrast to his brother.

My youngest would ask a homeless man, holding a sign, to borrow a dollar so that he could buy himself a Slurpee. Do not get me wrong, it would not be an attempt to be selfish. He would just merely see someone with something he needs, or wants, and ask him to share. Conversely, I have watched him give money away to people out of his own pocket without a second thought (only after his needs are met). When my oldest wants something, he gets pensive.

When he got quiet, I asked him a question men often dread, "What are you thinking?" As he is not yet fully a man, I figured the odds of the question getting answered were better than 50/50. As luck would have it, I was right. "Dad, can I have a hat?" My initial thought was that he wanted a baseball cap, but as we wandered into another store (or, rather, as I was dragged into the store), I realized he wanted a fedora. It seems that the fedora is all the rage these days – the modern day equivalent of the parachute pant (just significantly more stylish). The one he had his heart set on was a one-size-fits-all hat made of a tightly woven grey mesh (stylish and waterproof).

As we had just been shopping, and still feeling like the battle was mine, my first inclination was to say no. The more I think about it, my first inclination on a lot of things is to say no. Maybe that is something we evolve into as parents. We want to protect and teach. We layer in moments of safety and disappointment so that our children are better prepared. On the other hand, maybe sometimes we just default to "no" out of our own insecurities. I looked down into his blue eyes – my blue eyes – and said yes. To say he beamed when we left the store with his new hat pulled down over his bangs would be a gross understatement. He was radiant, he held his head up, and he walked with confidence.

There are any number of moments in a child's life when a parent can say they saw their child grow. Sometimes it is a physical change. Many times these are simply sentimental, but concrete, homages to the passing of time. What I saw from him in that moment was something more. It was sense of self that was not there a few months ago. It was more than the immutable passing of my time. It was the realization (for both of us) that time was quickly becoming his and he was willing to take it.

Some people might call the hat, and the desire to feel trendy, vain. Perhaps it is, but no more vain than my shoes. Sometimes forget that he is more than my son, he is a human being. He wants to feel cool, he wants to feel good – just like the rest of us. The longer I live, the more I realize that (at least for me) a sense of vanity is natural.

This leads me back to the battle. As he successfully expanded my scope, the casual reader might assume the battle to be leaning in his favor. Quite honestly, by the end of the trip, it did not matter that much to me anymore.

If we insist on settling the discussion – we could look at relative vanity purchases (I did try on the fedora, but it did not look right on me). He got his hat, but I have my Italian shoes. To that end, I think I still win on two points. First, there is the price differential. Second, and this is the trump card, they are Italian leather.

MANSCAPING

Pubic hair!
That is the second time I have started an essay with this phrase. I do not do this for shock value; rather, it is particularly, and unfortunately, relevant (as I am blessed with the rapidly maturing bodies of teenage boys). Realistically speaking it (the hair) is a simple fact of nature. The extent to which it exists is simple genetics. Some fight it, some embrace it. Many people in the latter category of these people reside in Berkley and annoy the hell out of the rest of us.

♋

I broach this topic for the second time because my sons make it impossible to forget that pubic hair happens. It is fascinating to the adolescent male mind at two phases. At first, its arrival signifies change, maturity and the evolution of a child into a young man. Boys, however, quickly realize it is often the defining characteristic of the female anatomy. This brings with it a whole host of additional changes (and often more laundry). Thankfully, I am still at the first phase.

There is very little privacy in my home. This is likely my fault. I have always encouraged my boys to be around, to talk, and to feel comfortable in my space. Often this leads to unpredictable circumstances. Occasionally, for example, they use my shower. As my home is small, I sometimes use their bathroom as an adjunct laundry room. They have little hesitation about walking into my bathroom to use the various facilities. For the record, my handbook on fatherhood did not cover casual conversations of a quasi-sexual nature while wet and lathered in the shower. I have had more conversations while showering than I thought possible. The rational human would think that children would respect the fact that you are bathing – these people, of course, do not have boys. Or, at least, they do not have my boys.

Realistically speaking, I do not expect my house to be overly ordered. I am not ordered, in either my mental facilities or physical space. As such, to expect my children to model an attribute I do not possess is illogical. However, if I have learned anything being a father, it is that your expectations of chaos pale in comparison to the reality of the impact a child has on your life. You (the father) are thinking it might rain today. Your children, on the other hand, are building an ark. They, in the end, are often much more prepared. While I do not expect privacy, I am often shocked at personal intrusions parenthood makes on one's life.

For example, one such intrusion is when you walk into your bathroom on a Saturday afternoon and there is hair piled on your counter. "Piled" may be a bit of an overstatement; however, in certain circumstances, there are not words to describe a spontaneous grouping of unwelcome follicles. The hair in question had been removed from the nether regions of someone in my household. As I was sure I had not, in a fit a sleepwalking hysteria, chosen to prepare myself for the average European Speedo, and I am quite sure my wife is more discreet, my only conclusion was that it was either a pubic hair elf (closely related to the elf that steals single socks from the dryer) or one of my pre-adolescent monkeys.

There was no point in my life when I thought I would ever be attempting to remove copious amounts of undesired hair from within three feet of my toothbrush. Further, I never realized that the adhesive properties of Velcro pale in comparison to random pubic hair.

Denial may be a universal trait for children. My sons, however, have elevated it to an art form that Da Vinci would envy. I asked them about the hair as emphatically as I could. I explained that their mother's eyebrow scissors should not be used for anything but their mother's personal grooming. All of this, of course, was to no avail, and I did not have the innate desire to perform a spot inspection to determine the ultimate culprit. If you think about it, the inevitable itching is really punishment enough. Knowing my boys, it may have been a team effort, and there are certain things that, even as a parent, you will never, and should never, know.

I often try to find a lesson in these small, life defining moments. The only wisdom I found is a realization that I do not know what to expect in life. Any assumption or attempt is pure folly. Beyond that, all I could take away was that privacy is truly a rare gift, and that you should always keep your eyebrow scissors under lock and key.

GREEN DAY IN THE FALL

I walked into my youngest son's room the other night. Even though they are getting older I find comfort in walking into each of their rooms just before bed. It helps me sleep better; and it helps me remember a time when they needed me sitting beside them before bed. These days, my youngest often puts himself to sleep. He gets tired, he walks into his room, he crawls in bed, and he sleeps. Many nights I walk in and find him snoring in the dark. I do not remember being that way when I was a boy. I do not remember ever really wanting to sleep.

♋

This particular night I found him lying there amongst his "things." He gathers things around him when he sleeps – he has long since outgrown stuffed animals. His radio is next to him on the bed – I think he likes the dim light and he loves to listen to music as he goes to sleep. He has a picture of our old cat that died in 2010. It is a digital picture frame, but he leaves the image on the cat – he loved that cat. The cat, on the other hand despised him. Cats, I think, tend to despise most people.

More than once I had to patch my son's arm from claw marks as a result of a bear hug to an old cat. It is sort of like the abominable snowman from the Bugs Bunny cartoons. My son would stroke him, and love him, and call him George. The cat was named Cookie and he seemed to really hate being treated like a George.

Next to the picture frame, on the bed as well, he has rocks. These are not just any rocks. There is a piece of "crystal" quartz, golden pyrite, and some other metallic crystal I have yet to identify. Finally, there are the mystery items. These are those things that he has taken an interest in or created recently. One day he created a sculpture out of nuts and bolts – I found that next to him one night. Tonight's mystery item was a pen that had a mirror on the end. It telescoped so you can look in tight spaces (like a car engine). I had found it in the garage and given it to him a couple of days earlier. As usual, he had everything on the bed within arm's reach. He slept facing his collection, calmly. He has always been Tom Sawyer in his soul, with bits of glass and rocks in his pocket. All he needs is an old door knob to complete the collection.

I often wonder what occupies his mind when he is sleeping with such a menagerie, but then again, his father is less than sane most of the time. So, I would suspect that the response would be the apple does not fall far from the tree. However, I have long since moved away from sleeping with pointy objects and electronic gear. Ultimately, he finds things he loves and adds them to his sleeping collection, and he does not like change. Really, the desire to hold on to things of comfort is completely sane. Nature, of course, does not agree. Nature is all about change. He has managed to adapt over the years. Even with the chaos that accompanies three cross-country moves, at his core he manages to still be him.

Having moved to California many years ago from Connecticut (a temporary way-point, itself), the thing I think we miss the most is the fall. I would take my boys on long drives from Fairfield County straight north and up into "New Hamster" (as they used to call it) to marvel at nature's transient palette. We do have fall in the Bay area – there are three to four days during late November when those deciduous trees supplanted from a more volatile climate are confused and decide that a dip in temperature for a few days means that fall is here. The other trees, I have no doubt, scoff at this premature and inexperienced one molting out of panic. This occurs in about February. Still, as much as I miss the fall foliage, having lived a portion of my life in Minnesota and spending a good portion of my time in Chicago, I have come to appreciate the delicate and nimble nature of California weather.

I think my boys miss the leaves as well. They would swim through piles of leaves as I cleaned the yard, and do their best to disappear into the mounds. My youngest, in particular, loved nothing more than to ensure that I never really got the yard cleaned. It is simply amazing how such a small body could redistribute leaves so quickly (and with such vigor) by diving headlong into the piles.

Of my two sons, my youngest is (currently) the one I lose the most sleep over. He sees the world very much like that pile of leaves. He smiles and dives headlong into conversations; he takes things apart to see what they are made of; he hugs you like a child hugs his teddy bear during a fall lightning storm. He is unique. Nietzsche said "The individual has always had to struggle to keep from being overwhelmed by the tribe. If you try it, you will be lonely often, and sometimes frightened. But no price is too high to pay for the privilege of owning yourself." That is a lesson he was never taught, he just seems to know it.

For 12 weeks this fall he has attended a special school, to learn "cognitive fluency." To translate, we just wanted to see him read. This is something he has never been able to do. To him, words are the antithesis of crystals, beads, and door knobs. They represent chaos, not comfort. To him, words are the brilliant leaves of fall. They burst into being, die in fiery color, and end up in piles as they decay away. So we drove him 45 minutes each way every day for 12 weeks so he could get six hours of individual instruction.

There is nothing worse as a parent than watching your child hurt, and not being able to do anything about it. As a man, I am supposedly genetically programmed to fix things – or at least I try. There are some things you cannot fix – they just simply are. A dear friend once told me that sometimes you just have to listen, wait, and let a problem work itself out. People that know me will realize how difficult this is for me to do. Last Friday, I sat in a cube at the "cognitive fluency" center and watched my son read a silly page of text about whales and dolphins. He struggled a little, but when he finished he looked back and me as if he were about to wink, and he smiled as if to say "I told you I would be ok." He then leaned back in his chair and put his arms behind his head. This, I think, he did just to spite me; I always make him put his chair down at home. All I could do was breathe, and smile.

Eventually, I drove him to the center for his final test (at least for now). The center is nestled in the foothills of the Santa Cruz Mountains. Fall was just winding down, so the trees along the way were at peak. I looked down at him and asked if he remembered diving through the leaves. He said yes, but I think he was just placating me. He was all smiles; proud, I have to believe, of what he had accomplished. Then he asked me for one thing – "Can we listen to Green Day?" This is something his mother would not have approved of. His favorite album is American Idiot, which is not the best theme or language for a budding literary mind. It is my fault (I introduced him to the music). I laughed, this caught me off guard. We drove down the road, trees exploding color around us with the phrase "I don't want to be an American idiot" blasting through the radio (both of us singing).

I often refer to feeling and experiences from

the perspective of a father. This is not to discount the experiences or feelings of a mother. For obvious reasons, my ability to reflect on the direct emotions of motherhood are limited. I say this because I am about to make a Gordon Gekko-like statement for both sides of this biological puzzle we call parenthood. Selfishness is good. Moreover, being a parent is about being selfish.

Everything you sacrifice is for those simple moments when your children make you feel that what you are doing on this planet is worth more than the breaths you take every day. Those simple moments are some of the most genuine in life. Singing Green Day in the fall was one of those moments. I have no doubt, Tom Sawyer would have approved.

LET IT BE

While I realize this will place me in a specific demographic, Solid Gold was my favorite show growing up. As a proper, barely-pubescent male, the weekly ritual of watching the Solid Gold dancers on stage was oddly arousing. At the time I did not understand arousal as anything more than an inborn physical flush that occurred despite your mother and father being in the room. Given the time, the level of clothing worn by the Solid Gold Dancers (or rather lack thereof) was both scandalous and remarkably cool. It was cool in the remarkably corny way that the 80s tried to make everything cool. It is as if Andy Gibb was one-upping Dick Clark in an epic Dorian Gray-like cage match, by saying "...you just have kids, I have women."

♋

Do not mistake my musing about Solid Gold as a yearning for the life of the 1980s. In respect to the 80s, I survived. I have some old records, and I generally do not speak of it beyond the occasional humming of an Air Supply song. Solid Gold came to mind because of a bike ride. On warm weekends, my boys and I would often take our bikes on a trail just behind my home that ran along the side of the Guadalupe River (which I used to mistake for a drainage canal). A few miles down the trail we would veer off and stop for a drink at Burger King. As simple as it seems, it allowed for a few quiet moments with my sons that I very much appreciated.

As they are growing into teenagers, I find that my time with them is becoming less and less (even when we are in the same house). For the cost of slushy, I get an hour to just watch them, and talk. The odd thing is that those small moments, when we are making small talk, are often the best of my week. On this particular Saturday, they wanted to ride ahead of me on the trail (another symptom of the sickness that is the teenage years). I let them go ahead of me, put on my headphones, and started my iPod. The song that came on was "Leader of the Band" by Dan Fogelberg. This song, of course, would lead any rational person to think of the TV show Solid Gold.

This requires further explanation (not that memories of the Solid Gold dancers need such explanation). In 1982, Andy Gibb performed the song "Leader of the Band" on the show. It happened to be the number four song on the charts that week; and, I remember that song being one of my very favorite songs of that year (or really any year). The Andy Gibb performance stands out in my memory because he got very emotional about the meaning of the song in his life. He dedicated it to his father, and sang. In my opinion, they should have had the Solid Gold dancers accompany him (they made everything sound better).

Over the years, that song (sans the Andy Gibb cover) has come to mean quite a lot to me. My father was not a musician. Actually, he was quite the opposite, an army colonel. But I still think of him whenever I hear it. I think of my father's life, what made him into the man he is today, and I often wonder about his passion in life. The odd thing is, I do not know and will not ever truly know what that is. To quote the song, "His hands were meant for different work and his heart was known to none."

As a son, I have often thought about my dreams and my passion in life. As a father, I constantly think of how my son's lives will be, and I ask them what they dream. The fanciful whims of childhood are spectacular. This week, being a pastry chef is in the mix. What we do not talk about is who I am when I am "off-the-clock" as a father. Perhaps we do not do this because I am not sure if I will ever be off that clock. Perhaps I do not have the answer. As much as I did not love Andy Gibbs version of the song, I respected the fact that he knew his father's passion, or at least seemed to.

For the record, I am a horrible singer. I know this; I have accepted this; and, I do not care. I still sing. I am not a shower singer (to me that is such a strange concept). I sing in the car. In my Cooper I can hit the highs of Freddie Mercury and be as smooth as Bobby Darin. My children learned long ago that when dad is in a musical mood, the only thing that they can be thankful for is that their friends are not in the car to hear a forty-year-old man (completely untrained and untalented musically) do his best impression of an Andy Gibb falsetto. On this Saturday bike ride, however, I just listened.

My youngest rolls his eyes and buries his head when I break out into song. I have yet to determine if this is embarrassment or sheer auditory torment. I thought for a while that it was simply the song choice. He proved me very wrong the other day. He is a Green Day fan, and when I broke out into the chorus of "21 Guns" while in the car, he looked as though he wanted to grab one of those guns and silence the fool in the driver seat. The only singing he has put up with (and many days begrudgingly so) is "Sweet Baby James." My children were both born while that song was playing. For years I sang it to them every night. Partially to comfort them, and partially to remind me of two striking moments of amazement, joy, and terrible fear that forever altered who I am.

The bike ride progressed like all the others. We stopped at Burger King, had our slushy, and rode down the grass hill at the edge of the park by my house. I left the song on repeat the entire ride back. It is strange the impact a song might have in our lives, and the tangible nature of the memories it brings. Some of the sharpest and most important memories of my life center on music. When the boys were young, and I lived in Connecticut, I would put Garth Brooks on "Callin' Baton Rouge" and dance crazy across a beat-up hardwood floor in my home while holding my sons. My socks would snag on the edges of the rough boards and the kids would just giggle.

Once your children reach a certain age, you lose your weekends. The days are filled with birthday parties and outings (that you are more obligated and obliged to attend). A day that starts with a leisurely bike ride and conversation often finishes in logistical chaos trying to get from one place to another. This particular Saturday was normal, and we moved from the bikes to the car and to the endless insanity that is a Chuck E. Cheese birthday party – I am not sure at what point we have deemed it socially acceptable to allow a rat to be the mascot of a food establishment. With the combination of food and rodents, there are few greater ironies in the restaurant business. I can only assume that since we are talking adolescents and pizza (marginal pizza), Chuck E. Cheese is a Switzerland of sorts for rodents and humans.

As we started our drive downtown, I turned on the car radio and was greeted with Paul McCartney singing "Let It Be." I looked at my boys in the rearview mirror, turned the song up, and started to sing. I think we all secretly sing to The Beatles when they come on (especially "Let It Be").

My youngest rolled his eyes (as expected). My oldest, unexpectedly, started to try to sing along.

As I looked back, he caught my eye in mirror, smiled, and winked.

I do not know if Dan Fogelberg ever talked to his father; I do not know if his father ever understood the impact he had. I suspect silent wondering is part of the job description most of the time. Sometimes, however, you can find the clues in the small moments. Sometimes you do not need a song.

For a minute I thought my oldest and I were singing together in the car. Looking back, however, I think he was singing back to me. In that wry smile and wink, we connected (at least for me) in the same way we connected back so long ago – dancing across that hardwood floor. It was a different song, but that did not matter. We are both older, but when he laughed in the back seat as the song ended, all I heard was the giggle.

BEAGLES ON THE TREE

" WHY did you slap your brother!?"
"I did not mean to hurt him dad, I thought he was asleep, and I wanted him to get up."

♋

There are few sounds in the universe like that of the bare right hand of a little brother connecting with the shirtless back of his older sibling. I am sure there is something similar, perhaps the sound a 3-meter spring board diver makes when he slips on a dive and performs the unintentional back-flop. This is only pure speculation; because, up to this point in my life, I must consider this sound unique. Unfortunately, at least in my house, it is not that rare. What happens next varies. Often it is the scream of the little brother as his offended larger sibling gets a hold of his hair, or his neck. Other times, it is the pounding of feet up stairs and the pitiful screams for help from mom or dad to protect him from much deserved retribution. In short, this is a typical Friday afternoon with two early teenage boys.

There really is no chapter in the parenting handbook that deals with this. I know, there are myriad books that wax philosophic about physical altercation and the proper parental response. These are similar books that explain the perfect way to make money in the stock market. Or, the one soldier who managed to run through No Man's Land and make it to the enemy trench without a scratch. The rest of us tend to get bloodied up a little bit.

Being home on Fridays is hit or miss for me. Often, I am traveling back from wherever my client has interned me that particular week. Or, I am at my office trying to avoid the next internment. This particular Friday afternoon was special – the day after Thanksgiving. In my house, that means the start of Christmas. Call me a traditionalist (and that would be a stretch in most aspects of life), but I do not like to really consider Christmas until I have eaten at least 3000 calories of carbohydrates in a single sitting.

While this was not a typical afternoon on the calendar, when it comes to brother versus brother relationships, there is no holiday truce. The scene is simple, younger smacks older in the middle of his back and runs screaming as his brother (after tripping over a couch cushion, which only makes him angrier) gives chase in their own unique game of duck-duck-goose. Today's game ends with older demanding that I slap younger in front of him. It is his idea of pre-Christmas justice. Instead, younger is imprisoned in a chair for at least 20 minutes, while I finish getting the decorations prepared. The chair is my Treaty of Versailles – no one within the geographical confines of the war zone really likes it, but the it stops the fighting, so we go with it.

"Twenty minutes!!! I cannot sit here that long, why?"

The fact that he says this with a smirk never fails to draw admiration from me (at least internally). The boy is determined, and once he is on course there is no wavering. Unlike most people I know in the world, he never second guesses his decisions. This, I think, will lead to more happiness than grief long-term.

"You have to sit until I can get the tree in place."

"We are decorating today!?"

I am not sure why this is a surprise, but then again, I am not sure why he is always surprised that he has to put his shoes on for school in the morning either.

"Like always bud."

I am not sure when I started calling the boys "bud." It seems so easy, in some ways more personal than using their names. It is almost like saying you are on some level my friend. I know, as a parent you are not supposed to be a friend to your child. But if you think about it, who else knows you on the same level your children do? It takes a spouse at least 20 years to learn to frustrate you the way your children can in well under ten. In that respect, children learn you so much better than most people in your life, and no one is better at using that knowledge for personal gain.

We have a fake tree. Years ago, we discovered that there were pine allergies in the house, so we switched to fake. All in all, I am happy with the change. I grew up with real, sappy, messy, scented pine trees. Sometimes I miss the devastation left by twisting a real tree up the front steps in through the narrow doorway and, ultimately, around the living room furniture and into the corner of the room. However, I have long since determined that my abilities with drywall patching are substandard. As such, my reminiscing about the look, smell, and process of a real tree are generally short-lived and finish with a lazy smile.

Once the tree is assembled and in place, my children descend like my beagles on a piece of steak dropped on the kitchen floor. If you have never seen this, it can only be described as cute, but determined, ferocity. Like the way Winnie the Pooh must approach the honey pot after the Lenten fast. He is still adorable, but something tells me the bear instincts will take over and I will lose an arm should I interfere.

In response to this onslaught, we learned long ago that ornaments need to be separated. There are those ornaments that the children get to place on the tree, and there are ornaments that my wife and I place on the tree. The ornament collection, however, is not separated solely based on fragility; instead, it is about memories. The boys do the majority of the ornaments – the ones they made over the years, the ones that speak to their lives, and the generic decorations. The other ornaments are reserved.

I travel quite a bit, I always have really. At this point in my life, I have been in over 18 countries and five continents. Sometimes these trips last a day, some have lasted months. I have lived in 13 cities and moved 22 times in my life. I am not pointing this out to brag, but, instead, to underscore the logic behind not getting too invested in too many physical things (they are hard to move). I am not a collector of trinkets; I tend to buy Christmas ornaments as souvenirs. There are ornaments and holiday decorations from every country I have ever visited and every place I've ever lived.

The adult box contains gold dipped maple leaves from the small house on the lake in Minnesota, a toy Mini Cooper (topped with the British flag) from London, a sea shell from a beach in San Francisco, an amulet found in a small shop in Scotland, a hand painted wooden egg form a vendor in Budapest, and innumerable, ineffable memories of sunsets the world over. That box the children do not get to touch.

"Do not bend the branches!"

If you have never worked with a fake tree, this statement makes no sense. On tree decorating evenings, it is a common refrain at my house. My children, in order to ensure that their placement is precise, and permanent, wrap the tips of the fake branches around the hooks or ribbons of the ornaments. This, of course, drives their mother crazy (as I said, less than ten years) as she always ends up removing the ornaments at the end of the season. Further, the art of having a fake tree is to keep some level of chaos to the vision – branches perfectly twisting into ornament shelves do not occur in nature.

Repeating the phrase about ten times during a standard decorating night is normal. This year it was 12; and while that is on the right side of the bell curve, it is nowhere near a record. The alternate chorus of most decorating evenings is, "I do not see any on the front of the tree. Spread them around." It only had to be said six times.

"Where is the pickle, Dad? Are we doing the pickle this year?"

Every family has traditions. Some are created as an overt choice, others just fall into place. Years ago we got an ornament shaped like a pickle. On Christmas Eve, long after the boys are asleep, the pickle gets hidden somewhere in the bowels of the tree. The child that finds the pickle on Christmas day gets a special gift (usually a special candy bar). I have been told that this was a tradition that started in Victorian times. Honestly, I have never researched the origin, and I do not care. My boys always ask for the pickle game, they remember it with joy, even as they grow older and magic grows less magical. Anything that helps a child see mystery is a tradition worth holding on to – regardless of the origin.

"Dad, I have more stuff to place on the tree. Hold on, let me get it!"

My youngest collects things. These things might be shiny rocks, old door knobs, costume jewelry, Legos, or really anything that fuels his perfect imagination. When he really loves something, a person, or a process, he gives his treasures away. It is not uncommon to see his dog (Mason) adorned with some crystalline structure hanging off the collar – "doggy bling" as it were. It is the most sincere sign of love, but there have been occasions when the dog displays pure indignation at the additional weight on his neck. If you have never seen it, beagles are good at indignation, not cat-good, but in the dog world they are indignation champs.

The resistance to additional Christmas tree bling (that which is better suited for the collar of the non-indignant beagle), is often the last battle of most tree decorating evenings. The battle, as expected ensued, and it interrupted the Carpenter's Christmas album. Karen Carpenter means Christmas in my house. I cannot start decorating the tree without first putting on the Carpenters Christmas album. Years ago my mother would play that tape over and over and over in her little blue Mitsubishi. I thought I hated that music back then (I got tired of it). Today, it is all I want to listen to at Christmas.

It makes me think that maybe some things we do as a parent do sink in, the battles notwithstanding. I cannot, of course, tell my mother this. I was a son before I was a parent, a good fight is a good fight and there is no sense in giving up, even when your mother is right.

Post tree decorating euphoria is usually marked by my children retreating to their rooms (or the basement) and their Xbox communities.

For me, I like to pour a glass of wine, turn the lights off in the room, look at the tree, and think back across the years hanging from the branches. This year, hanging just above center, off to the upper left and then to the lower right, are multiple porcelain beagles. These represent the boys most prized possessions – their dogs, Mason and Spencer. They came into our house as Christmas gifts years ago, and they have invaded every family moment since. It was inevitable that their likenesses would end up on my Christmas tree.

If I were a song writer, I could try to amend the standard Christmas carol to remove the partridge from the pear tree and replace it with beagles. They will depart from my life many years before my children will (God willing), but the ornaments will be there reminding me of evenings filled with Karen Carpenter and fights to keep the branches from getting twisted around the ornaments.

I have boxes for my sons, simple dark wood boxes. When they leave my side one day – be it to their own families or to place their hearts in the hands of the world – they will get those boxes filled with a few ornaments. They will each get a cloth snowflake, a gold covered leaf, a porcelain beagle, and a Carpenters CD. Those can be the start to their sacred ornaments, the ones that provide the moment of peaceful, happy reflection every year. As a parent, I realized long ago that I can only give them a start to the collection – the remainder they have to find for themselves.

ALMOST MEN IN TIGHTS

There are few times in a man's life when he can wear spandex – with any level of confidence. I admire those men, the ones that stand proudly on the beach in their Speedos (often with bellies covering their more delicate parts). There is the occasional Adonis that puts us all to shame, and simultaneously makes us believe that we too can look like Dolph Lundgren or, more recently, Ryan Gosling. These are differing body types, but I would be happy with either. And there are also few times in a man's life when tights are suitable. Middle school is not one of these times.

♋

My oldest son recently joined his junior high school wrestling team. He did this, according to him, to make me proud. Truth be told, I probably influenced him in this direction. My fervor was less about wrestling and more about keeping him active. Tights never crossed my mind. My wresting knowledge is limited. There is a lot of sweat, and a wonderful movie was made about it in the 1980s. I remember this movie more because of Linda Fiorentino than the wrestling theme. I would suspect she is why most men might recall that film (unless you prefer Matthew Modine). I have seen interviews with Matthew. He appears an eloquent conversationalist and is fetching in a suit. Even so, he is not my type. Furthermore, none of this figures into the motivation for my son.

From a parent's perspective, the instance of a child's selfless motivation adds pressure. When your child does something directly at your behest, you feel you are on the hook for their joy. It is like recommending that experimental Dutch film to a good friend (the one who likes Woody Allen movies, so you think guttural Dutch is in the ballpark). When they come back disappointed, you realize that you have just revealed way too much eccentricity in your personality. Not to mention, they will likely never go to a movie with you again. There is also a good chance that restaurant recommendations will forever be ignored (especially that Dutch-Cambodian fusion place).

Wrestling is a quirky sport. The wonderful feeling you have when your child comes home from practice and tells you how much fun he is having quickly dissipates when you see him sitting stone-faced and sullen at his first match. He is going to get on a mat and fight (in a manner of speaking) another human being. There are rules.

It is only to pin or to win on points, and there is limited blood or injury. Nonetheless, if the boiling anticipation I feel while watching other young men face battle (knowing my son is next) is anything like the apprehension he must be feeling, then stone-faced is simply a mask for sheer terror. Another explanation for his look (equally likely and terror inducing) might be that he has to eventually take off his shorts and T-shirt and stand before the entire crowd in a singlet.

A singlet is an interesting piece of clothing. It can only be described as a cross between lederhosen and child's "onesie" (manufactured in the same fashion of Spanx). Singlets have a short-like look, but pull toward the top of the body in a way that cinches and accentuates the bumpy parts of a man. Eighth grade boys have lots of bumpy parts. As maturing males, some of those bumps are where you would expect; others, are just sort of there, along the torso, in seemingly random locations – proportion and the early adolescent male body are very much strangers. Further complicating the matter, many eighth grade boys are proud of their bumpy parts, and seek to protect them. The sight of a skinny child wearing an abnormally large athletic cup beneath the singlet is something to behold. If you got him to lay face down and hold a plank position, you could use him as a teeter-totter. My son's turn came to step on the mat, his singlet exposed. I stood up, camera in hand.

The ensuing 20 seconds were a blur. The world stood still, I was not breathing, and I could hear my heart beat in my ears. I know it was 20 seconds, because he was pinned (with seemingly no effort from his Spartan-like opponent). Exactly 20 seconds had expired from the official clock. He got up from the mat, shook the other boy's hand, and looked up at me, almost in tears. All I am thinking is Dutch art film.

I wanted to yell out that it is ok, that I loved him. But, demonstrations of overt tenderness are not welcome in a testosterone laden auditorium. I smiled at him, mouthed words to let him know I was proud, and watched him walk back to the bench.

Progressive parenting will say that it does not matter that he lost (that winning or losing is irrelevant). In the mind of an eighth grade boy, that is garbage. Participation trophies do not impress eighth grade girls, and why else would a boy wear a singlet? One positive note for my son, and not so positive for my rapidly beating heart, this was a multiple school match – he had another chance. I closed my eyes, took a deep breath, opened them again, looked back down at the mat (and at the next set of monsters walking over to wreak havoc on my psyche), and settled in.

It took another 20 minutes for him to get his second match. In that time, every kid on his team was pinned by the opposing team. I can only imagine how demoralizing and unnerving it was for a 14-year-old boy to sit and watch and realize he has to step in next. His match time arrived; he stood up, and checked-in at the judge's desk. No one from the other team joined him. It turns out that the other team did not have someone in his weight class. The referee walked him to the center of the mat, raised hand, and let him walk off – winner by forfeit. To my surprise, he did not smile. He looked up at me with utter disappointment.

He did not smile, it turns out, because he wanted to show me how good he was. He wanted to show me what he could do. I love my son. He has done wonderful things in his short life; and, he has done some not so wonderful things (I have had to patch the holes). However, I do not think I was ever more proud of him than I was in that moment. He just wanted to compete, to be part of the match even when the odds were not in his favor. He would rather have lost trying rather than receiving a quiet, effortless victory. I do not think I took a breath for 40 seconds.

We talked all the way home. We talked about winning and losing. We left it simply – you'll lose more than you will win – that I know. I have been there. Winning is easy. We all like it. Even still, I told him, you should know the taste of losing. It is like lima beans, no one likes them, but they are good for the body and soul in small doses (or so I have been told).

No more wrestling movies for me, this weekend I think we will try "Das Boot" together. It is not Dutch, but it is a good film. I might even buy an adult sized singlet for the occasion.

UNICORNS AND TRAMPOLINES

The concept of joy is fleeting.

Further, I do not think a parents experience with joy is completely unique. Joy, or at least the transitory nature of it, is a human condition. One exception may be the Amish. They seem to be happier than most, but then they have really good butter; and in the pyramid of happiness, good butter leads to good cookies. Cookies are a higher order joy inducing food (this is one of Maslow's lesser known, but important, philosophies).

☙

True joy, that moment when you stop thinking and revel in the feeling, is rare. If you have teenage boys, then the likelihood of finding that moment is on the same fairytale scale as the quest of a hero that must get the tear of a unicorn to save his one true love. His love, by the way, may well be a frog in need of the unicorn tear to become a real princess again. This scenario is possible, in some universe where unicorns exist, but it is more than a little rare. Do not mistake my sentiment, there is utter happiness within children (even teenage boys), it is just a very rare moment when you (as a parent) can revel in their happiness and completely let your guard down.

For example, there was that moment at the trampoline park. The concept of a trampoline park, in and of itself, is one fraught with disaster. Gathering a group of pre- and post-pubescent boys in a closed space, putting them on trampolines, and telling them to play dodge-ball is a bad idea. It starts out well-intentioned, and as the father you feel yourself drifting into a state which must be reminiscent of nirvana. You are playing with the kids and you feel like one of them. You are being accepted into that alternate fairytale universe. You watch your son make a diving catch, and, in mid-air, deflect another projectile away with the one he just caught. It is a moment that you expect to see on Sports Center that evening. You jump away, still looking back at your son, let your guard down, and start drifting into that joyous euphoria. It is at that moment that you (while flying from trampoline to trampoline) crash into an eight-year-old boy.

For the record, children bounce. Better still, children on a trampoline bounce even higher. The bouncing helps defray injury. Also, once the air has come back into their lungs, they do stop crying. You, on the other hand, with your sense of joy now safely tucked away, realize that trampoline dodge-ball is not a good mixed-age activity.

Watching your children in sports of any kind leads to a lot of these almost joyous moments. A year ago, my oldest took up running. There are far worse habits he could undertake for a love of a woman; and, there is the irony of him actually chasing after her. In respect to distance running, my son is not fast. He comes by this naturally – I am not fast. He made it through cross-country (literally chasing behind her), and as spring arrived, so did track season. He went out for track – she did not.

To my surprise, he did not stop. He joined the team, went to practice, and by and large seemed to forget about the girl. This seemed appropriate (given his age). He ended up as a sprinter (this seemed inappropriate given his genes). Again to my surprise, it turns out he is actually decently fast (in my family, we have taken to calling this the rogue unicorn gene). Even so, "decently fast" and being a freshman means you will lose a lot. His season was about establishing personal bests, finding pleasure in the team, and learning that sometimes you surprise yourself more than anyone. He seemed to find joy in all of it. I was traveling during the last meet of the year. He had a personal best in five events. Being a father means that sometimes you have to miss those moments – it is in the job description.

The funny thing about joy is that you cannot will it into existence (at least, this is not a skill I have mastered), but sometimes it slaps you in the face unexpectedly. The day after his last meet, my oldest begged his coach to let him go to sectionals. His personal best was not good enough to qualify, but he wanted another week with the team. He wanted to run. Ultimately, his coach entered him into the meet, simply to give him the experience. He was not official, but he would get to run.

The week of sectionals, I was in three cities and barely made it to the meet (15 minutes to spare). Taking my place on the rail, camera in hand, all I could see where boys looking like (what I perceive to be) elite track athletes. There was my son smiling among them in the infield. In my head I am singing the old Sesame Street song, "One of these things is not like the other..." The first heat for the 100-meter dash started, my fear piqued, and the boys streaked by. The first heat for the 100 was run, and the two qualifiers finished with times of 9.95 and 10.1, respectively. When his heat arrived, he stepped to the line and waited for the gun. Heart throbbing, I waited. The gun sounded.

The winner of his heat finished in 10.06 seconds. Four seconds later my son crossed the line. If you are unfamiliar, in the world of track four seconds is somewhat akin to 40 points in basketball. Looking down at the track, I saw him turn and jog back to his lane at the finish to get his official time. He looked up at me, a beaming smile from ear to ear and gave me double thumbs up. He had made it to sectionals, he had run his race, and he was joyful.

Sometimes, as a parent, I think we get obsessed with the search for happiness, for success, for joy. That day he made me think that just maybe a sunny afternoon and being part of the game is enough. Maybe it is enough to just know unicorns exist, and seeing them even in that fleeting moment lets you find your own magical tears.

However, it is important to remember that magical tears do not work on trampoline dodge-ball injuries.

IN THE END

What scares me most about my children is that I fear they will not find passion in anything. I went to a Beatles tribute concert one Saturday night. I went with a best friend from childhood. Oddly enough, when we were children, I did not realize how close we would become. I have other friends from that time. We still talk regularly, but he has clung to me like a brother over the years. He has seen me when I am my happiest, when I am silly with laughter, and no portion of time muddies my vision. As such, I find great joy in seeing him.

♋

The band we saw was called Rain. Generally, I do not like tribute bands, but it was a birthday gift. Further, this group was significantly more refined. They have played on Broadway, toured through Chicago, San Francisco, and other major cities. They were excellent, and I got to forget the world for a night.

I have been a fan of The Beatles my entire life. I remember growing up in the late 70s, in Las Vegas. My neighbors (older teenagers at the time) would have me come over and listen to Beatles albums. The Beatles, in my mind, should always be played on a cheap record player. There is something very special about the crackle of the needle moving over the uneven vinyl surface of Abbey Road.

Abbey Road was the first album I ever bought. I took five dollars down to the grocery store on the corner and bought the album from the discount rack. It was a beautiful, semi-reflective, black satin. That record was the most mesmerizing thing I had ever seen (of course, until I picked up the White Album – that was crazy impossible). The fact that those little grooves could produce such a wonderful sound still perplexes me to this day. I may have grown up, but I never lost my love of The Beatles.

I sang every song from the audience that night, and I smiled like I did when I was 10-years-old. Looking back, the smile was the real gift. The concert was just means to an end. Now, looking at life after 40, I find myself missing those records. It is time, I think, to start reclaiming my collection (with a better record player).

When I go to shows, musical or otherwise, I like to read the biographies of the performers. The members of the band, Rain, had spent large portions of their lives studying The Beatles (and music). They knew the mannerisms and the voices – but a skilled actor can learn these. What was most interesting was that they were all highly accomplished musicians. Each had been studying Beatles music since they were 12 and 13-years-old. In some sense, they found their passion early; and they spent much of their lives pursuing it.

My sons are just slightly older than I was when I found passion in that music. They are slightly younger than the members of the band who did the same. Logically speaking, there is no need for them to find their life's work when they are still standing at the edge of childhood. But, this is the worry of a father – who, ironically enough, has changed passions innumerable times in his 40 years.

Still, I can remember looking at the world from the age of 12. I have distinct memories from Laurie Lane – of riding my bike, of playing with my first computer, of losing my father to the world, of moving into puberty, and of the white oleanders that lined our back yard like poisonous, delicate guards. I knew nothing of passion. Really, passion is something that I have only found in the last decade of my life. It is selfish to think, or desire, my children to find it faster. But a worrisome father can only hope. I remember seeing the world at 12, so I cannot hold my breath.

It is also, I think, natural for a father to look back across his life and forward into where his son's might go. There is no lack of experiences waiting (at any age).

Twenty-one, for example, is an interesting age. I did not get carded on my 21st birthday. When in university, this (of course) is the only day you want to get carded. I got carded the day before my 40th birthday, but not on my 21st. That is good karma coming back to me. I cannot say I know what I did to deserve it, but where the universe is concerned, any attempt to understand is ridiculous. What struck me about 21, looking back now, is that I was not afraid to dance then. I would go out to clubs with friends from the dorm and dance, drink cheap liquor, eat salty popcorn, and then end up back at the dorm playing cards until 4 a.m. By that time, however, some of the weariness of life had found me. Some nights the music slipped away, but I could still find it most days. I cannot say that I knew the world then (especially looking back with my perspective now).

There is a kid (I have to call him that) that I worked out with – Harry. We spent 18 months taking martial arts together. What I remember most of Harry is his smile. Even at 21 (he was that age the last time I saw him), he smiled like he was 10. He would swagger into the room with that silly grin almost every night. He had the music still, and I cannot imagine he ever lost it. He died at 21, killed as a Marine, a kid in Afghanistan. I cannot speak to his passion – I would like to think he simply lived it for as long as he had. But he reminded me of seeing the world at 21.

At forty, I look at the world much differently than I ever thought I would. Strange, but not only have I found passion (in unexpected places and people), but I am finding joy in a sense of accomplishment. There is a gentleman (I will always call him that) that I worked out with as well – Steve. He was a quiet soul, 42 at the time I met him.

What struck me about Steve was how much joy he felt. He made a promise to himself at 40 to get his black-belt. That promise drove him. He would commute an hour to the studio before work every morning and smile while he worked out. His smile was not that of a 10-year-old. Instead, I think now, it was the smile of simple satisfaction in knowing that he had learned to navigate his world. Perhaps that is the most profound thing about 40 – you feel some level of control (illusory or not). Steve died at the age of 49. I received the news on the morning of my 40th birthday. He died of cancer, surrounded by his family. Learning to look at the world from 40, I smiled for him that morning.

Looking back at 12, 21, and 40, the one constant thing I can discern is that passion is fickle. I envy those musicians who found there world in music when they were so young. We all pretend to be someone else most of the time – for those artists, there is joy in it. I wish that level of joy on my children and can only hope they keep Harry's smile for many more years than he did. Of Steve, I know there was love in his life and a level of peace – I wish my children that as well. For me, I still strive for passion – I am a senseless romantic, but not stupid one (sometimes obtuse, never dense). I have promises to keep and I can only hope that ultimately The Beatles were correct:

"...and in the end, the love you take is equal to the love you make..."

AFTERWARD

The astute reader may have caught all of the musical references throughout the text. For the record, the author was not so astute when writing it. After reading through the essays, my editor (whom I find very astute), mentioned that she liked how I used music to highlight many of my stories. Music has always been an inspiration for me; but, until I went back through the text myself I did not realize how many songs I call out in the book. Specifically, I directly mention or allude to 15. Funnier still, the mix is as eclectic as the essays themselves. Given that we live in the age of social media, and almost instant access to music, I thought it would be fun to provide you with my Hair, Girth, and Rude Awakenings playlist:

"Sweet Baby James" – James Taylor
"American Pie" – Don McClean
"Silent Scream" – Richard Marx
"Still Your Song" – The Goo Goo Dolls
"Waiting For My Real Life to Begin" – Colin Hay
"My Heart Will Go On" – James Horner & Celine Dion
"Leader of the Band" – Dan Fogelberg
"21 Guns" – Green Day
"Callin' Baton Rouge" – Garth Brooks
"Let it Be" – The Beatles
"Merry Christmas Darling" – The Carpenters
"Only the Young" – Journey
"Golden Slumbers" – The Beatles
"Carry that Weight" – The Beatles
"The End" – The Beatles

ABOUT THE AUTHOR

Mike Nader is a freelance writer and software consultant who has lived in seven states, and three countries. Over his career, Mike has spent time teaching junior high school, selling roofing products, and working in the software industry. He has coauthored two books on technology solutions, and has been a closet essayist and poet most of his life. Mike lives outside of Chicago, Illinois with his wife, two sons, and two beagles.

MICHAEL NADER

9 780692 259726